AWAKE

josh groban

ISBN-13: 978-1-4234-2476-5
ISBN-10: 1-4234-2476-X

HAL•LEONARD®
CORPORATION
7777 W. BLUEMOUND RD. P.O. BOX 13819 MILWAUKEE, WI 53213

Visit Hal Leonard Online at
www.halleonard.com

CONTENTS

MAI

Music by LEO Z. and ANDREA SANDRI
Lyrics by MARCO MARINANGELI

Non guar-dar – mi; non cer-ca- -re di spie-ga- re. _____ Lo sa-pe-

YOU ARE LOVED
(Don't Give Up)

Words and Music by
THOMAS SALTER

Don't give up;_____ it's just the
Don't give up;_____ it's just the

weight_____ of the world._____ When
hurt_____ that you hide._____ When

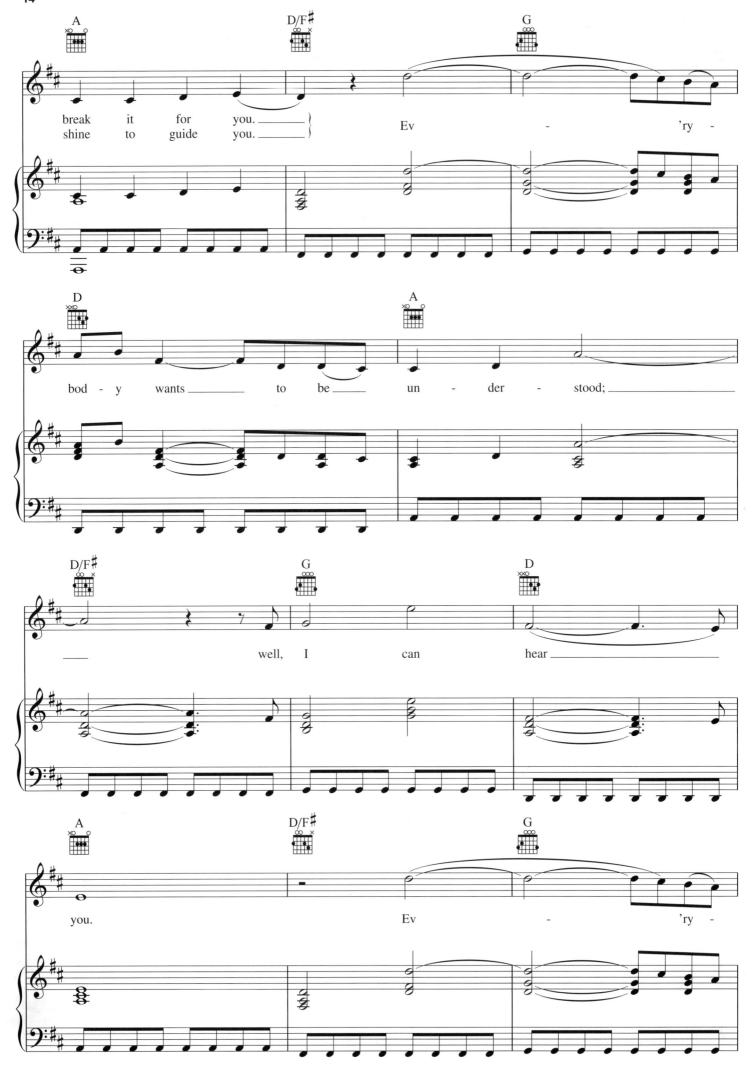

UN DIA LLEGARA

Music by OKSANA GRIGORIEVA
Lyrics by CLAUDIA BRANT

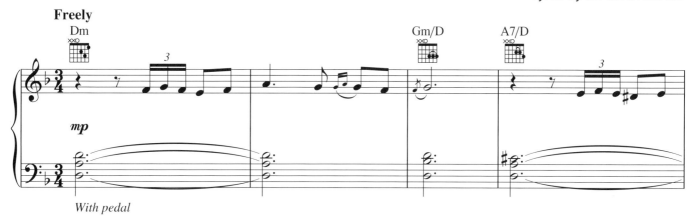

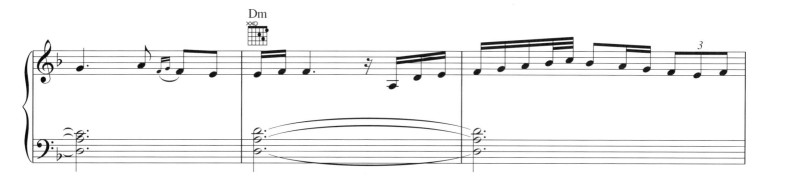

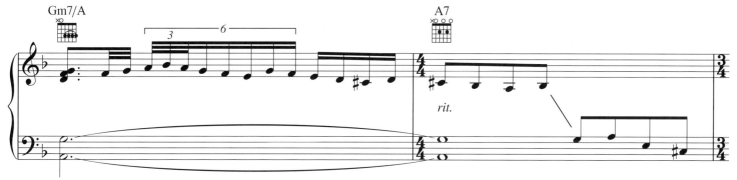

lle - ga - ras.

FEBRUARY SONG

Words by JOHN ONDRASIK and JOSH GROBAN
Music by JOSH GROBAN and MARIUS DE VRIES

(1.,3.) When all that I've ___ known _____ is lost ___
(2.) Some - times it's ___ hard _____ to find ___

_____ and _____ found, _____

my _____ ground, _____

___ I prom - ise you, I _____

'cause I keep on fall - ing

L'ULTIMA NOTTE

Music and Lyrics by
MARCO MARINANGELI

*Recorded a half step lower.

SO SHE DANCES

Words and Music by ASHER LENZ
and ADAM CROSSLEY

waltz when she walks ___ in the room; ___ she
waltz for the girl ___ out of reach. ___ She

IN HER EYES

Lyrics by MICHAEL OCHS and JEFF COHEN
Music by MICHAEL OCHS, JEFF COHEN
and ANDY SELBY

*Recorded a half step higher.

eyes, time pass - es by and she is with _____

me. _____

SOLO POR TI

Music by MARK HAMMOND
Lyrics by MARCO MARINANGELI

Di - me que ha - rí - a   de   mis ___   dí - as; ___
Di - me   lo   que   sien - te ___   tu al - ma; ___

quien so - ña - rí - a   si   no es - tas?
di - me por - que   vi - ve en mi.

*Recorded a half step higher.

NOW OR NEVER

Words and Music by JOSH GROBAN
and IMOGEN HEAP

UN GIORNO PER NOI

from the 1968 Paramount Pictures film ROMEO AND JULIET

Music by NINO ROTA
Words by LAWRENCE KUSIK and EDWARD SNYDER
New lyrics by ALFREDO RAPETTI a/k/a CHEOPE

Slowly, with freedom

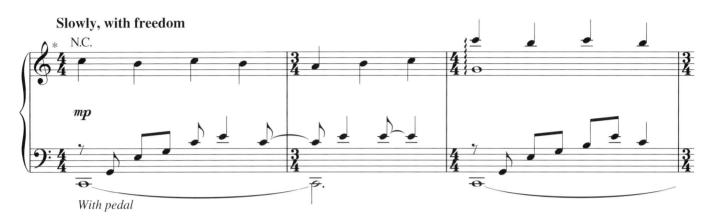

*Recorded a half step higher.

LULLABY

Words and Music by JOSH GROBAN,
DAVE MATTHEWS and JOCHEM VAN DER SAAG

*Recorded a half step higher.

WEEPING

Words and Music by DAN HEYMANN,
TOM FOX, IAN COHEN and PETER COHEN

*Recorded a half step higher.

* A Zulu proverb meaning "Man can only do so much."

MACHINE

Words and Music by JOSH GROBAN,
DAVE BASSETT and ERIC MOQUET

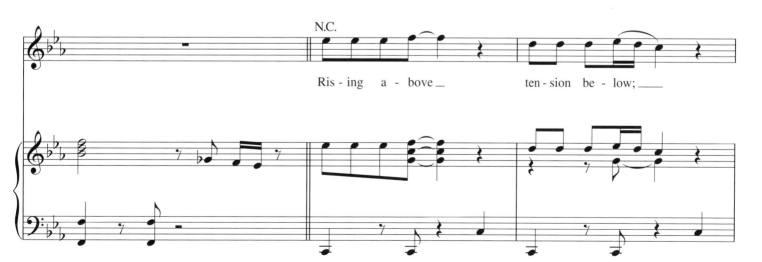

Ris - ing a - bove ten - sion be - low;

heart, _____ oh, _____ there's no _____ heart, ___ and I've

spent all this ___ time feel - ing some-thing you can't feel at all. ___ You're a ma-chine. ___

Oh, ___ you're a ma - chine. __